Married 2 An Addiction

Marietta Mills Jones

Married 2 an Addiction

4Ever Thankful, LLC
www.4everthankful.com

All Scripture quotations, unless otherwise indicated, are taken from the King James Version.

Edited by: So It Is Written
Email: info@soitiswritten.net
On the Web: www.soitiswritten.net

ISBN-13: 979-8-218-38410-4

Contents

Foreword

When I first met Marietta Jones in March of 2008, I was certain that she didn't like me. I was hired into a role where we would be working closely together. She was professional, but reserved, quiet and secretive. I had no concept of the burdens she carried. I mistook her distraction and need for privacy for her personal dislike of me.

Over time, trust grew between us. We opened up to each other a bit about our lives, losses and shared Christian faith. Our relationship deepened to a sisterhood, and I soon began to understand her furtive phone calls and unexpected time out of the office. Her work never suffered a whit, but I could see weariness growing in her. It worried me. In truth, I desperately wanted her to leave her husband Bernard and care for herself.

The morning Marietta called my home to share the horrific news of Bernard's death, I was stunned. I feigned calm, asked pragmatic questions about what she needed, and pledged to pray for her. But I was shaken. I could not comprehend how anyone could absorb such a violent loss of the love of her life—on top of the violent loss of a sister and a previous fiancé.

In the days that followed, Marietta demonstrated grit, grace and unwavering faith. I was in complete awe – from her motivational words of praise to God at Bernard's memorial service – to her brave face when returning to work. She remained private and reserved. Again, I misread her. But this time, I mistook her demeanor for strength and self-sufficiency.

In this inspiring book, Marietta displays great courage and characteristic humility by sharing her pain, vulnerability and unflinching self-examination. We gain insight into the experiences that led her to marry Bernard, the attachment to hopes and dreams that kept her entrenched in a cycle of misery and the internal struggles that she bore alone in her quest to rediscover herself and to find peace and purpose in spite of great loss.

Marietta's earnest insights give us a better understanding of the anguish caused by addiction – whether to drugs or unrealistic ideals – and hope for peace and growth. In an age when society is fraught with addiction, anxiety and depression, Marietta shares her path of discovery and example of fearless introspection, all under the umbrella of an unwavering faith in God. Faith is the thread that runs through every aspect of her life and love. And, with an honesty that few would reveal, Marietta shares how even her faith – or her perception of what faith should be – became a stumbling block and threat to her very life when she didn't lean fully on God's understanding.

With a clear voice, Marietta admonishes women not to lose themselves in relationships – and to remain true to themselves and a *personal* relationship with God. She also gently reminds us to minister to each other in times of loss – even to those who seem strong and self-sufficient.

I've watched Marietta on her incredible journey. She has taken each step with grace and gratitude (so much so, that I think of her every time I see her watchword, "thankful"!) It's been a joy to watch her blossom, when I didn't think it was possible for her soul to become any more beautiful.

The lessons in this book are plentiful. The applications to everyday life are endless. Marietta has assembled wisdom worth reading and absorbing many times over.

It occurred to me as I read the last page of this book that Marietta's dream was to minister to others with Bernard. And, in a way no one could have predicted, she is doing just that by sharing their experience and her subsequent journey to encourage, enlighten and inspire.

I'm so proud of you, my sister, and I honor and love you forever.

Tina Creguer

Introduction

The best place to start is with the truth.

So many times, we can defend what we believe, then justify our actions based on what we believe. However, oftentimes, what we believe is a lie that we've created in our own heart to keep from facing the reality of our choices. It's easier to say, "I did this because of..." rather than face the reality that, "I did what I did because it's what I wanted to do." The cold reality is that when our choices do not produce the results we want, we always find an "out." Eventually, the very thing we built our hopes on comes crashing down around us and almost destroys us.

We all make choices that have the potential to break us down, but glimpses of hope (or what I like to call "beauty marks") can be seen, even at the ugliest points. The question I had to ask myself is, "What should my next move be? More specifically, should I stay, or should I go?"

This book was written at what seemed to be the end. In reality, it was the beginning of a special phase in my life story. I went through so many things naturally, spiritually and physically on my journey. Of the many questions before me, I've always asked myself two main questions: "Why did I stay?" and "What was the purpose of it all?"

You may think you know the answer. However, I'd encourage you to wait until you hear the whole story before you make a judgment. Even though my "cross" may have been a loved one's addiction, many of us have situations where we had to make hard decisions.

I ask that you prayerfully read this book to see—not just my situation—but how the choices that we make are just that: *the choices we make.*

God is faithful to His Word and He loves us unconditionally. Because of our "free will" to love Him in return, He doesn't make us love Him. Instead, He allows us to experience His love, which in turn causes those who embrace that reality to love Him back. Even as a believer who walked in that unconditional love, I made many choices over the years that were not proper responses to His love. I made the choice not to love. I could argue that I didn't know what I was doing and that I acted out of ignorance, which was sometimes true. But I could have also acted out of arrogance, pride, my own ego, or from a religious mindset.

The addiction I talk about in this book is not the addiction that people might think about when they hear the word. I started writing this book in the middle of, what I now like to call my "beauty marks" rather than in the middle of my husband's addiction. I don't like to say "his addiction" because I don't believe it was something that defined who he was, nor did it have ownership over him. It did not belong to him.

I thought I was going to write a book about him and what we went through as a couple. I thought that the book would have a triumphant ending, where he got off drugs and served diligently in the ministry. He had a passion for ministering and mentoring others. I believed that's how the story would end.

But the story did not end that way … *or did it*? I invite you to walk with me as we hear what the spirit of the Lord has to say to us. I pray this book is a blessing to you. I pray it serves as a tool of self-evaluation. This open book of my life story isn't for judgment or ridicule of others, which may indeed come. The purpose is for us all to take a close look at ourselves and not "pass the buck" when we are hit with the ugly circumstances of the life that manifests from the choices we've made.

The Day My Life Changed

It was Sunday, September 27, 2009, around 10:30 a.m. Suddenly, there was a knock at my door. I had just finished getting ready for church. We were having a bake sale, so I was putting the finishing touches on my famous cream cheese mini pies. I thought, *Bernard must've lost his keys.*

When I opened the door, I was greeted by a male and female detective from the Detroit Police Department.

My immediate thought was, *What in the world did Bernard get himself into for the Detroit Police to come looking for him over 30 miles outside the city in Farmington Hills?*

Once inside, they asked me several questions. "Ma'am, do you own a 2008 Ford Focus? Who was the last person with the car? What time did the car leave your possession?"

Puzzled, I answered the questions in the order in which the detectives asked me. "I am the owner of the car. My husband, Bernard, was the last person with it, and he left home around 2 a.m. What's going on?"

Instead of responding to my question, they continued asking more questions. "Could anyone else have taken the car? When was the last time you spoke to Bernard? Do you know where he was going?"

Things still didn't register with me.

"I haven't heard from him since he took the car last night. I don't know where he went."

"Ma'am, is this normal behavior for Bernard?"

At this point, I had to be honest with them. I replayed the series of events from the previous night.

That weekend had been one of the best weekends since we'd been married. We celebrated our fourth wedding anniversary on Thursday, September 24. We had a beautiful dinner as we spent the evening thanking God for allowing us to enjoy another year together.

Here is what Bernard posted on his Facebook page as a tribute to me: September 24, 2009
"I just wanted to say at 3:10 a.m. Happy Anniversary to my wife. You are not only the best wife that a man could have, but you are also a friend. Your love,

concern, sincerity and strength are unmatched. I thank God so much for you and I pray that we live to see forty more blessed years. The devil is a liar and so are his supporters. God withstands every storm and accusation brought against His people. Jesus said, 'Upon this rock, I build my Church and the gates of hell shall not prevail.' His Word is always true because we have seen hell in more ways than one. We always said that we wanted to glorify God through our union, so let us both thank Him together because He holds all things together. I love you, beautiful woman. And I wish the best and same for all married folk. And by the way, I'll be a much better husband and man this time around because you deserve that and much more."

On Friday, September 25, 2009, we spent the evening at a married couples' event at our church. This was our first time at the event. We had so much fun fellowshipping with other married couples. The one thing that stood out to me was the game we played. It was like speed dating. There was a long table, with each couple sitting across from another couple. Within a certain amount of time, each couple had to say how they met their spouse and why they loved them. This gave me the opportunity to hear from Bernard how much he loved me. I never doubted that Bernard loved me, but God knew what was to come. God knew I would need to have that moment embedded in my heart.

On Saturday, September 26, 2009, Bernard and I spent most of the morning together with my mom at the Detroit Zoo. Then, we went out for lunch as an extension of our celebration. After lunch, my mom and I dropped Bernard off at his cousin's house around 3 p.m. I picked him up around 11 p.m. That night was different in so many ways. He had been drinking, but he hadn't exhibited the typical behavior he had after drinking. He was never violent or mean to me during those times. However, I could always tell when he had been drinking.

I also knew that drinking was one of the things that triggered his desire for drugs.

Once we arrived at home, he went into our room, took all his clothes from the closet, and set them on the couch. He wanted to get rid of everything that was connected to his past. He wanted to start over again. Since the onset of his addiction, this was the longest period he stayed clean. So, when he pulled all the clothes out, I didn't think anything of it. He was calm. He wasn't anxious, which was normally a sign that the addiction was rising within him. I could always tell when it was on him. So, I did things to distract him. I did all I could to remove any temptations from him, such as hiding the car keys and his wallet. This time, he didn't show any of the normal signs. Therefore, I simply listened to him and encouraged him in what he wanted to do.

While in the kitchen, I heard him turn on the radio in the living room before he went to the bedroom to remove more items. He wanted me to go with him to take the clothes to our nephews, James and Chris.

"It's too late, Bernard! It's 2 a.m. We can do it after church tomorrow."

He agreed, yet he continued gathering his things.

He came back a while later with six shoeboxes.

"I'm taking these to the dumpster," he said. "I'll be right back."

Little did I know, that would be the last time I would see my husband.

After five minutes, I went outside to check on him and found that the car was gone. I went upstairs to check my purse and discovered that my keys were missing. I realized then that he'd turned up the music to distract me from hearing him go through my purse for the keys. He didn't take any money or my bank card. Just the keys. I got mad, but I'm not sure if I was mad at him for drinking, or mad at myself for missing the signs of the addiction and not hiding the keys.

At this point, the addiction had been going on for two and a half years. It wasn't until eight months prior to this that I was able to have total peace that God had everything under control. I finally realized that I could not change him or deliver him. Bernard would have to yield to the finished work of Jesus Christ at Calvary. Yes, God loves addicts, too! After I stopped being mad, I went to sleep. I knew I had to attend church in the morning, and at this point, I trusted God for his life. Because we only had one car at that time, I knew he would come home. He always came home.

After hearing the summary of events prior to him leaving home and hearing more about his addiction, the detectives told me the reason for their visit.

"Ma'am, your car was found in northwest Detroit in a vacant lot on fire—with a body in the trunk."

Still puzzled, I looked at them with a blank stare.

They asked me again, "Ma'am, do you know if anyone else could have taken the car?"

"Bernard did not have money. He would rent the car out for the night in order to get drugs. This is more than likely what had happened."

"Ma'am, the body we found was burned beyond recognition, so we can't say if it's Bernard or not. You will have to go to the morgue tomorrow to identify the body."

Once the detectives left, I notified Bernard's family. We searched for him in the areas I knew he frequented for drugs. Because God had given me such a peace over the eight months leading up to this day, I never imagined that the body in the trunk was his. Even on my way to the morgue, I didn't believe it was him. When we arrived, we couldn't even view the entire body because it was so burned beyond recognition. The only way we could confirm his identity (without an autopsy or consulting dental records) was from his tattoo. The body had been laid on its side, so his left arm was on the carpet of the trunk when they found him. It was the only part of his body that was not burned. The tattoo had his brother Mike's birthday. Mike had preceded him in death due to complications from drug use. When his brothers confirmed the date, we knew it was him. I think I was in denial—not just that day—but for months afterward because I'd never saw an actual dead body.

Years later, I found myself driving in those same areas where Bernard frequented to do drugs, hoping that the police had made a mistake. But they hadn't. I would even entertain the thought that he had somehow faked his death to start a new life and get clean so that he could come back as the man of God he knew he could be. Regardless of the facts, I constantly battled in my mind that my husband—who always came home—was not returning home this time.

Chance Encounters

I met Bernard through his mother, just before the death of her oldest son, in April of 1994. His mom and I served in ministry together. She was like a godmother to me. I spent more time at her house in prayer and worship than I did at my own home.

Bernard was in prison at that time, nearing the end of an eight-year sentence. Concerned for her son, she asked ministers to write him letters throughout his sentence to keep him encouraged. I was one of those ministers. Bernard took the death of his brother hard, and not being able to come home for the funeral was even harder on him. Through the letters I sent to him, we became friends.

During this time, he was a minister in the Nation of Islam. He knew the Koran backward and forward, as well as the Bible. He always debated with me and asked me questions about the Bible. "How can The Trinity exist? What's the whole dynamic behind that? Does it make sense?" He was very argumentative. His mother said that she knew, when he was a child, that he was either going to be a preacher or a lawyer. He always had a lot of questions and he always sought answers. He was very inquisitive, sharp and smart. Anything he put his mind to, he excelled at beyond measure.

Bernard spoke his mind. He said what he wanted to say, but he spoke the truth, even if it was about himself. We had lengthy debates about Scripture and his belief system. The Nation of Islam is a dominant religion among African American males in the prison system because it gives them a sense of identity that the outside world can't give them. In prison, these men are finally recognized as strong black men. This is what Bernard wanted—to been seen and heard.

In his book, Bernard said, "I had people praying for me on the outside while I was incarcerated, but it didn't mean anything. It was the same old thing to me. I was already witnessing people that only ran their mouths but would never produce. So, I became a militant, Black Nationalist, hateful man. At least now I had a way to vent my resentment. But I would later learn that this too was only a learning experience."

When he came home a few years later, our heated conversations continued. Because I'd established a relationship with his family prior to him coming home, I looked at him as I did his siblings. They were my family and so was he. He didn't like that. I never thought of him in any other way because he was really irritating. He always challenged me to, "Be ready always to give an answer to every man that asketh you a reason of the hope that is in you with meekness and fear" (1 Peter 3:15).

As we interacted more, he saw me as more than a sister. He often told me, "You're going to be my wife."

I told him repeatedly, "That will never happen because we are family."

Slowly but surely, Bernard shared intimate parts of his life with me. Being raised by a single mother, Bernard didn't like the men who were in his mother's life telling him what to do. He also didn't want to watch the physical abuse she endured, so he left home as a teenager. Because he felt like he wasn't getting the love he needed at home, he looked for it in the streets. His father, "Butch" Jones, was alive, but was absent most of Bernard's life because he was one of his mother's abusers.

Under the influence of the men he hooked up with in the streets, Bernard began selling drugs. Eventually, he started using drugs, as well, to impress the other men. While the other men simply used to dibble and dabble in drug use, Bernard's compulsive behavior meant that he went all out. So, he became addicted to the very thing he used to make a living from. He told me stories of when he was homeless, finding food wherever he could and sleeping in abandoned houses. The very people whom he thought loved him were the ones who turned their backs on him once he was no longer able to produce a profit for them.

He recounts a significant part of his story in his book. "Due to choices I made, whether willingly or unwillingly at a young age, I spent eighteen years incarcerated. Prior to incarceration, I was already in bondage at an early age. I was introduced to drugs at the age of twelve by a man that I looked up to as a hero. Due to this habit, it caused a great deal of low self-esteem, rejection and even a feeling of hopelessness at an age where I should have been playing on a playground. I was ostracized by family, friends and even by myself. This produced, at an early period in my life, an attitude that said, 'Whatever!' I was marked a long time ago by not only the devil, but by people, to be destined to be nobody or even dead. I saw drugs, shootings, killings, violence and dysfunction. This was a norm and it was okay with me. I was pretty much on my own at the age of thirteen. Not because I didn't have a family, but because I had Satan and he had me.

I found myself in and out of jail until one day I was finally sent to the adult prison. Here I was, coming from bondage to yet another level of bondage. Every problem that I had grew larger. I hated prison, as well as the people inside of it. I felt lonely, distant, scared, empty and crazy all at the same time. By this time, I hated my family more than I hated anything else, besides the prison guards. I had to live in that place with uncertainty every day as to whether I would live to see the next day. I often wondered if I would live to one day finally be somebody worthwhile. But nothing changed. I became bitterer and my soul's hole only became larger" (Jones, 2009).

When Bernard came home from prison the first time, he got hooked on drugs again. Me, his mom and his godbrother prayed for him, and he was able to walk away from the drugs. He did go back to prison—not for drugs this time—but for trying to support his girlfriend and her newborn child, which wasn't his. Because he wanted a family, he took on the role as the father of the child and head of that house. When they needed money, he did the only thing he knew how to do from his years on the streets. He robbed two young ladies at gunpoint. Because he was a repeat offender, he was sentenced for six to eleven years behind bars.

I went to court with his mother when he was sentenced. Turned out, the prosecutor for his case was the same one who had prosecuted the three young men who murdered my sister in 1990. I had a chance to speak with him and pour out my heart on behalf of his mother. However, because he had a long juvenile record and prior time in prison, he had to go back. As you continue to read, you will see where my need to "fix" everything came from.

During his second prison sentence, he became angrier at everyone: family, friends and, even at one point, God. He felt like his family should bear some of the responsibility for the choices he had made. When his family didn't, he alienated himself from everyone. It wasn't that we didn't want to be there for him, but he had to take responsibility for what he did, not us. We loved him, but he had a view of what love looked like. When he didn't get love in that way, he thought we were the bad people.

At one point during his second term in prison, he got on my nerves so much that I stopped communicating with him for a year. He couldn't understand why the only person who had once stood with him abandoned him. I was concerned about his relationship with Christ more than his relationship with me. I felt in my heart that he used his anger against me and his family to blame others for his choices.

During this silent time, he met a Christian and gave his life to Jesus Christ. Because of his compulsive nature, he went full force into studying the Bible and developing a relationship with Christ.

This transformation is what birthed various writings I later compiled into a book and published on his behalf after his death, *In My Own Words – My Life's Journey from Beginning to Eternity*.

"At this very moment, I sit here with a mind that is full of confusion, doubt and unbelief. These things have happened to me in large part due to sin and rebellion. But God has a way of taking things and making them work together for the good to those that love Him and are called according to His purpose. Yes, I knew God and served Him with my entire heart, yet and still, I fail away. My hedge was removed, and I cursed God in my confusion and sickness. But I thank God that, despite this, He's bringing me out. In bringing me out, He also allowed me to learn a great deal about the hearts and souls of His people" (Jones, 2009).

I was at his mom's house when he called her to tell her that he had given his life to Christ and that he was getting baptized. From that day on, our relationship was rekindled, but on more of a spiritual level. In the past, I could not talk to him without getting into an argument. By this point, I could sense a true peace in his heart, even with him knowing that he had many more years ahead of him.

"Prior to being released, I received the Lord in a way that was so real that I was convinced. I came home a man sold out to Jesus, with the desire to do nothing more than to serve Him. But now the hedge was removed, and I would be tested" (Jones, 2009).

Once he became a Christian, we both shared a common passion. Our conversation was no longer combative, but it was filled with faith and hope. Where I was once irritated with him, I now looked forward to our conversations. Since he had studied the Bible as a Muslim, he was now able to connect what he learned to not just words written by man, but love letters written to reveal who God is and His will for mankind. I have two large binders of letters from him on revelations he received from God. The peace he had been looking for in family, friends, the streets and drugs had been fulfilled in his relationship with Christ. We spent hours on the phone sharing our experiences and love for God and His people. This is when I saw him as a *man*, not my *brother*.

He stirred something in my heart that my spirit had longed for!

When I realized I loved him, I called his aunt and cried. He had told me, since the first day we met, that I was going to be his wife. Even though I was dating his godbrother, and I knew he was a "bad boy," he never changed his story. How could I fall for someone like him, and while he was in prison at that? The crazy thing is that I never considered his past at this point in our relationship. Nothing about his past drug use entered my mind. It was as if it had never happened.

Once I shared my heart with him, we communicated more about God and our future. We solidified our love for each other with him asking me to marry him in the prison visiting area.

The one thing he wanted to do was move away from Detroit once he was released. He wasn't afraid to face his past, but he wanted to start a new future somewhere far away from his family. I didn't want to leave because of my mom, and I think I was somewhat fearful of leaving my job, as well, since I was uncertain of his ability to get a job once he was released. After all, who would hire a felon? Because he loved me, he decided to stay in Detroit once we were married.

However, that turned out to be the worst decision of our lives!

Side note: Ladies, if you are willing to marry a man, you must be willing to submit to him and his leading. That's why the man you marry should have a love for Christ. That way, you know his decisions are Christ-led. Ephesians 5:25 (AMP) says, *Husbands, love your wives [see the highest good for her and surround her with a caring, unselfish love], just as Christ also loved the church and gave Himself up for her.* Had I allowed him to be the man of the house and followed his lead, he may be alive today.

Before coming home from prison, he wrote me a poem titled "My Heart to Yours." It explains his perspective of our journey starting from when we first met, to his time in prison, up to the point of his transition home.

"The first moment I saw you, my heart skipped a beat. Who is this mystery woman that stands at my feet? 'Marietta who?' my mind inquisitively asked. Is this woman spoken for? I found out she was, but I didn't really care. There was something about her.

"So, I attempted to get closer, but only got so far. This woman is good, but she doesn't know who you are. So, I tried to use my street knowledge to gain a point or two. But the Holy Ghost covered her. What was I to do?

"This woman is spiritual, and I'm a slave to sin. 'But my game is tighter,' I thought. 'So, in due time, I'll win.' But the more I tried to get closer, the more evident it became that her mind was going in a particular direction and mine had to do the same.

"But sins feel so good, and it's all I've ever known! 'It's that kind of attitude,' I thought, 'that will stop her from loving you.' Where did that thought come from? Maybe because I had heard it before? I didn't know then that Heaven had something greater in store. So, I left that thought to itself, along with the woman I admired so much, and dated this girl called sin, that made me shiver with a touch. And in no time at all, this other girl would prove to be true, that the wages of your sins will catch up to you. 'But I thought you loved me!' I said to sin in her face. What do I get from this relationship, besides sitting in this place? She said, 'The wages of sin you surely know is death, so there ain't no need in calling me because there ain't no love left.'

"So now I sit in a room, turned out and used, for chasing what I perceived was pleasure that left my soul bruised. All alone, being tormented day and night by memories called demons that left me with no sight. I called out to Allah but didn't hear a word in return. There go those demons again, 'Burn baby, burn.'

"When the enemy had me to the point where I lost all hope, God's ministering angel appeared and simply said, 'Hope!' Hope is not lost if you turn to Jesus Christ, and the good thing about it is He comes with no price. The price that was demanded, He paid with

His blood at a place called Calvary. Now that's much love.

"What are you talking about? And please identify yourself. I'm that mystery woman that you laid on the shelf. But here I am again, with the same message and intent, to share what I know about Jesus, hoping this time you'll be convinced. Bernard, you don't need me. What you need is Christ. He will be everything you need in this wretched world called life. If you would only stop torturing yourself, and blaming others for your plight, and call out for the name that's been exalted above all others, you'll get through the night. So, she closed her letter with a Scripture or two. There I sat alone, wondering what I should do.

"Confused and misguided, not knowing what to do, I didn't choose Jesus. Instead, I chose you. But with you being guided by God, and being filled with His spirit, the message I sent your way, you just weren't with it. I tried everything I knew and became frustrated in my endeavor. I threw up my hands and just said, 'Whatever.'

"So, a silent period came, and you were nowhere to be found. But little did I know that my change would come around. One by one, things began to disappear. I cried out for help, but no one was near. Affliction after affliction came rushing in like a mighty storm. But with each hardship came a revelation, and this wasn't a norm. I looked to others to help deliver me from this mess. But that's when the word came to me, 'It's time to confess.'

"'It's time to meet Jesus. That's what this drought is all about. And the wilderness is used to bring that about. You see, the Lord needs you broken with a contrite heart. The suffering you face, son, will set you apart. Just the way I want you, all to myself, consecrated for My purpose and no one else. It's time for you and me to sit down and talk and allow me to reveal through my Word the way you should walk.' So, I confessed with my mouth, 'Jesus Christ is Lord, and was raised from the dead by the Father above.'

"When I opened my eyes, everything was so clear. Endowed with power from on high, and the ability to see things as they are. The Word took on more meaning, so now I know who you are. I rushed to the water to be baptized in Christ. And when I arose from the water, I went looking for my wife.

"I am a covenant child and Abraham's seed by faith. Blessed with every spiritual blessing that ushers me to a new place. The day that I stepped out of the baptism pool, I jumped on the phone. And to show how all things work together for good, you were at my home. Filled with the Holy Ghost, and the power of his might, being in your presence, was still out of sight.

"The Lord reached down in my spirit and brought out something that had been buried for so long. A prayer that said, 'I want this woman,' and never felt it was wrong. So, He spoke to your spirit and you sensed something inside. The next thing you knew, you jumped in your ride to see what took place. Has this man truly changed? Comparing spiritual things with spiritual, a confirmation you received indeed. God has begun a new thing, our spirits both perceived.

"'Where do we go from here?'" is the question we both asked. Let's keep acknowledging the Lord, who will direct our path. So, we turned to our Savior, with much prayer and fasting. And received the self-same revelation, 'You've arrived at last.'

"Begin your journey together to become one. For your relationship in love will typify the Son, the Son's relationship that he has for His church. A love that's sacrificial and means so much.

"So, as we piece this union together, let this mind be in us which is in Christ. With every decision we make, we won't have to think twice. Let's not look at divorce statistics or what the critics may say. Instead, let's keep our minds stayed on God, knowing He will lead our way. As the head of our house, I will be led by Christ and bring nothing but sweet blessings into your life. He who finds a wife finds a good thing and gains favor from the Lord. So, together we sing; sing a new song, like Solomon did because the birth of our relationship is like having a kid.

"God has shed love in our hearts by the Holy Ghost, which is given us. A love that's so divine that says, 'In God we trust.' So, we both become an expression of God's love. So, when we look at each other, what do we see? God loves you and He also loves me. The race is not to the swift, but for those that endure. The foundation of God forever stands sure. So, as we walk together, in this divine union from on high, allow the image of the Son to be transformed to you and I."

He said all these things to speak into my mind, body and soul! I didn't verbalize it, but in my heart, I felt like I'd hit the jackpot!

Once word got out that we were planning to get married, the people who knew Bernard had been in prison, and those who knew about his drug addiction, questioned my sanity. Interestingly, his family was excited for us and gave us nothing but encouragement and love. They knew me for years and they knew I would love him. They knew I would walk with him as he continued to grow in the things of God. I don't think they thought we would get married so soon after his release from prison, though. I don't think anyone did. Even with that, they stood with us and prayed for our union.

Having those who supported us constantly tell him how awesome our union was going to be helped fueled that inward desire to have the perfect marriage.

Little did they know that my desire really wasn't to get married, but to have the fantasy I'd always dreamt about come true—which was to marry a man who loved God and do ministry together.

The Tale of Two Worlds

Even though Bernard and I found common ground around our love for Christ and each other, the "elephant in the room" was still there. We both ignored it, as so many other people do in the name of love. He and I literally came from two different worlds.

My sister and I were raised in a home with both parents. My mom was a stay-at-home wife until we were in high school, and my dad worked on the assembly line at Chrysler. He was also a deacon and Sunday school superintendent at a small Baptist church on the eastside of Detroit.

I followed my dad everywhere; he was my hero. I was the youngest of his ten children and I was spoiled to no end! He was born in 1913, so I was raised with old-school rules. He had his first daughter at the age of sixteen, seven more children in his first marriage, then my sister and me in his second marriage. He lived an awesome example before me. My dad and I were the first people at church and the last people to leave.

My whole life from the age of my youth was ministry. I loved God and reading the Bible. I was intrigued with the story of Solomon and how he prayed. He had the opportunity to ask God for anything. Rather than asking for riches and wealth, he asked God for wisdom and how to rule the people in his kingdom (1 Kings 3:1-14). So, I always prayed, "God, give me wisdom." He always did. But somewhere, I mixed my will into God's will, which took me on a course I never imagined.

Kind of sounds like my sister Eve in the Garden who wanted something outside of God's original plan (Genesis 3)!

Even though I lived in a loving home with two awesome parents, I always felt like I had to make them happy. I always did everything my parents told me to do. I may have questioned their requests as an adolescent, but as an adult, I respected them and did whatever they told me to do, the first time. This was true in just about every area of my life.

I believe this is where I started losing my identity.

Even though I grew up in the church, and I had a love for the things of God, I found myself questioning what I believed after my sister was murdered in December of 1990. Leading up to her funeral, friends and family talked about how she lived and enjoyed her life. She had fun and was an outgoing person.

Listening to them, I pondered, "What would people say about me at my funeral, except that I went to school and went to church?" That was my life.

The same month of her death, I purposed that I was going to have fun and enjoy life. From my twenty first birthday in December 1990 to February 1992, I was pretty much out there. I didn't do drugs, but I hung out, became promiscuous and drank a lot. There were times I left parties and had no clue how I got home. It truly was the grace of God on my life.

On February 14, 1992, I turned my heart back to Christ. I realized that He had not left me. He still loved me, even though I'd willfully chosen something else to fill a void that only He could. Just as my sister's life was taken, I was putting myself into life situations where others could have been taken, as well.

I also had to ask myself whether I was truly a Christian before 1992! I knew God and I knew the Word of God. I was aware of His love for me, but why had I been so easily swayed by an "image" of a life I thought I should have before I died?

The dots were beginning to connect!

During my time of "being out there," I dated Renard Lee Davis. I had known Renard, AKA Nardy, most of my life. I grew up down the street from his grandparents. On my birthday in 1991, we got engaged. He was a small-time weed distributor. When I gave my life back to the Christ, I broke up with him. I told him that I loved God more than I loved him. We had been intimate. But, at that point, pleasing God was greater than pleasing my flesh. There was no need for us to stay in a relationship.

When he saw that I was serious, and that I was committed to my Christian walk, he desired to stay in the relationship. He loved me and could not imagine his life without me.

He stopped selling weed, went to back to school for his GED, and continued to get a certification as a welder. He changed his whole life just to be with me. But in August of 1992, he was an innocent bystander in a drive-by shooting in front of his sister's house. I was there, as well.

The internal bleeding from that incident messed up his lungs and, eventually, he needed a lung transplant. While in an induced coma for a month, he would periodically awaken and tell me that he loved me. Because we were engaged, his family allowed me to be listed as next of kin. So, when he became critical, the hospital called me. That call I received reminded me of the call I answered at my parents' house from the city morgue to identify my sister's body.

"Ms. Mills," they said, "we are having a hard time keeping Renard alive. So, we advise the family to get here as soon as possible to say your goodbyes." My pastor at that the time took me and his grandmother to see him at University of Michigan Hospital in Ann Arbor. Once there, I had a chance to tell him that I loved him. I also prayed for him before watching him take his last breath on August 31, 1992.

After losing my sister and the man I loved, I engulfed myself in ministry. Dating, or the thought of falling in love again, never crossed my mind. Thirteen years later, Bernard came along. I've always believed that there is a purpose behind meeting someone. So, knowing that he was a Muslim, and knowing some of our differences, my sole purpose at that point was to minister to him. There was no other purpose for our relationship in my mind.

As a woman, there were some things I desired because I had been in church most of my life and God promised me those things in His Word. Even though I wasn't dating, I knew it was better to marry than to burn. As an ordained elder, my concept of marriage was not only to marry a man who I loved—but also to serve in ministry together. We would win souls to Christ together. That "image" I had, which I conjured up in my mind at the time of my sister's death, caused me to see my life through the lens of these self-defined "images" instead of my reality.

Nowhere in the Bible did God promise all that! As believers (those who believe the Word of God), we can't manipulate the Word of God to meet our needs and desires. Yes, He wants the best for us and will provide it. But we can't tell Him what that should look like based on our own personal agenda.

We often have this idea of what we want in life. If someone speaks wisdom into our lives (which may be from God), and it connects in any way with the hidden desire or image within us (which may not be from God), we often take that spoken word in a completely unintended direction.

What was my ultimate motive in getting married?

Whatever choices we make in life, we must live with the consequences. I can't blame anyone for all the things I went through because I chose to be his wife. I did all those crazy things in the name of love. I could have waited to get married.

Could my desire to be the wife of a great man of God have been because of my hidden agenda to be great? Thinking back, my desire to be great in the eyes of people was my driving force, maybe not the actual marriage.

Could it be that I saw the potential in him, and I was willing to work with him to help him meet that potential? This is not necessarily a bad thing, but you should never dim your light for others to shine.

Was there something in me that made me feel like I was doing something honorable or praiseworthy because I was helping him?

Had my desire to always please my parents as a child been the catalyst, which took me off the course of who God created me to be? I know that God is all-knowing, but these thoughts often overtook the reality I knew about God.

Home Sweet Home

Bernard was released from prison on August 30, 2005. We married September 24, 2005. I planned the wedding once we got his release date, but I didn't send invitations out until he arrived home, just in case the prison changed his release date.

Even though we were in communication for over thirteen years, we only dated, hung out and interacted outside prison walls for 26 days before getting married. During marriage counseling, the pastor asked, "Why the rush?" I assured him that I wasn't pregnant. Bernard felt like he had wasted so much of his life that he didn't want to wait to begin the life he had always dreamed of, prayed for and envied.

While in prison, he had studied carpentry and electrical work. His desire was to build and repair homes. Within a week of being home, even though he was still on parole, he had three job offers! The blessed part is that they were all in the field of carpentry. He had favor beyond what either of us could imagine.

This was our sign that God had blessed our union!

I'd always dreamed of being married. I dreamed about packing my husband's lunch for work and leaving encouraging notes to remind him throughout the day that he had someone at home who loved him. I think I watched too much TV and soap operas. So, when we did get married, I did just that because he worked so hard and was so proud of what he did. I wanted him to know that he had my support and love.

Thinking back to that period, there were several red flags that made me question if we were moving too quickly. It was nothing that he did physically. It was just something I felt within myself.

The first red flag was that I felt God telling me to wait. I didn't feel that I *shouldn't* marry him, but the timing wasn't right. Since I'd worked on this wedding for months, and I had already sent the invitations out, how could I go back to people and recant my statement: "God told me he was my husband."

This man loved me, and I knew in my heart that he would do what he could in his power to be the man God called him to be. I saw glimpses of this, but from a distorted view. I wanted to be married, but I didn't want the marriage itself! Time showed me that there is a difference.

"Getting married" points to the overview of a perceived notion of what that means. This could be why you might question the sanity of a woman who would marry someone abusive or marry someone who is a narcissist. The image of "getting married" outweighs the reality of how the "marriage" may play out based on the realities that are right in front of us.

We wrote letters to each other and read them in our wedding program. In my letter, I said, "God anointed me to be your wife." I had no idea at the time how true and prophetic that statement was. Bernard had so many unresolved insecurities. He was trying to prove to his family that he'd turned out better than what they said he would be growing up. God had placed me in Bernard's life to constantly remind him of who God created him to be, but little did I know that I didn't have to become his wife to do that.

The day after our wedding, I got a bottle of champagne to celebrate our union. His past never crossed my mind, so I didn't think there was anything wrong with it. However, I believe that champagne awakened something inside him. Having been locked up for so long, alcohol wasn't a demon he had to face—until I brought it back into his life. There were many days that I wondered if I played the role of Eve by encouraging him to partake in something that ultimately changed our lives.

The Pains of Ministry

Despite his past, Bernard loved God. Years prior to coming home, he was a diligent student of the Word of God. Anything he could get his hands on to learn more about the Word, he did.

Once home, before the addiction, he was elevated to the pastor in the church we attended. Even then, I felt it was too soon for him to have that much responsibility. However, because he knew the Word and was able to articulate it in a charismatic way, he was promoted to the pastoral role. He quickly realized that the ministry he knew in prison was totally different from the ministry on the outside. This was the first distraction that caused his mind to go back to his former life. He struggled with the fact that what he read in the Word of God didn't line up with what he saw in those who confessed to be Christians. Because Bernard was a vocal person, he expressed his feelings, which weren't welcomed by many.

"I learned fast that there was a difference between inside (prison) and outside in terms of the church and believers. I came home, wanting to grow and serve, but I ran into Hollywood. I already had my own demons, unbeknownst to me, but running into the things that I saw in the body of Christ only agitated those unhealed parts of me.

"I came home to what I discerned to be idolatry in the church. Although the language was Christian, the spirit was something different. I was being asked to bow to Jesus by way of bowing to the personage of a man (preacher). I made it clear early on that I wouldn't do this, so I was labeled as a rebellious brother. No, I wasn't rebellious. I was hearing from God, the same God who said, 'My glory I will not share with another.' I saw unholy things. I allowed my family to be used by those who served their bellies. As a young believer, this was confusing. I saw the same game being manifested on the pulpit that I'd seen on the street corners and in prison with pimps, dealers and killers. Call it what you may, it was a familiar spirit, but I still saw it. I tried to talk with believers and leaders, but instead would only be marked as a troublemaker. Yes, it got to the point where I became a troublemaker because I wasn't equipped to deal with this in the spirit because I was a babe in Christ."

Once his addiction was exposed, many in the church turned their backs on him. Many thought he had no right to speak against what he perceived in the church because he was messed up. They didn't feel like he was qualified or justified to speak on such things. I did all I could to keep him focused on what he needed to do to stay clean. I kept my mouth shut on a lot of things concerning ministry, even though I was in total agreement with him on most points.

"I saw the church being used like the army, following the familiar slogan, 'Be all you can be.' Church had become a place that was only a substitute for the nightclub, drugs and late-night booty calls. I saw people who could not grow in the ministry because they didn't have immediate benefits (finances) to those who served their belly. I saw the way people and ministry names were being exalted over the One who lived, died and rose again. I saw the way ministry gifts were misused and held up as idols. I saw people appear as though they had power over the way the Holy Spirit moved and performed in the lives of God's people. I saw what God alone holds and controls in His hand being supposedly released by others. I saw the gifts of the Spirit being patented and monopolized by others who desired to keep people running to them instead of Jesus."

Bernard was very vocal about this and spoke out boldly on this topic, which caused division between him and his family. Because I saw this as a distraction for him, I would not voice my opinion either way on his view of the Church. I felt my position was to remind him of who he was and to help him not focus on others' flaws, which he had no control over.

The Addiction

The definition of addiction according to dictionary.com is: (noun) "the state of being enslaved to a habit or practice, or to something that is psychologically or physically habit-forming, as narcotics, to such an extent that its cessation causes severe trauma."

In the early days of our marriage, amazingly, everything gelled. We both finally had what we had dreamed of and prayed for in a marriage. It was almost as if we had known each other forever, or we had been hanging out with each other for years. We knew each other's personality, likes and dislikes. Everything flowed well for that first year. Everything was perfect. It wasn't anything we tried to make happen; it just flowed naturally. *Or did it?*

The beginning of his addiction was crazy. I didn't understand it. I'd never been around anybody with an addiction, other than that brief encounter with him before he went back to prison. I had never been around him in the middle of his addiction. I was never around him when he was high or getting high. So, I didn't know the depth of what that does to a person or to people who see it.

The first day I learned about the addiction, Bernard did not come home for almost 24 hours. He had never done this before. I called hospitals and the police. It wasn't until I called his brother that we figured out what happened. His brother asked me to check our bank account, which never crossed my mind. When I did, I saw the various transactions and withdrawals from the account. I immediately called the bank to have the card canceled, thinking someone had stolen it. However, by that time, every dollar was gone. His brother explained to me that this was a sure sign that Bernard was back on drugs. His family knew the signs because they had seen him throughout much of his previous addictions.

A day later, Bernard came home in tears. I had never seen him cry before. It scared me because I saw how hurt he was. He told me how he had been out all night, smoking crack. He said that the thing that hurt him most was that he didn't know why he did it. He knew the damage it could create. Before, he did it because he felt worthless and unloved. But, at this point in his life, he had everything he wanted—including a wife whom he knew loved him. So, it tore him up that he'd opened a door that he swore he would never enter again. I did all I could do to console him. I reminded him of who God created him to be. I quoted just about every Scripture that I could think of in that moment. This was just the start of his addiction, though. Little did I know, another one was being birthed at the same time.

"I spent many days in the streets, wandering, scared and lost, without any care in the world. Many times, my own wife had to come and pull me out of dangerous territories. Thank God for a loving and believing wife. It was this very woman that God used so many times to comfort me and remind me of the love of a Father. Sin isn't worth all you will lose and all that you will encounter! I spent many days in bed, being tormented by the multitudes of demonic spirits. Oh yes, God is much more real to me today. I spent many nights crying, shaking, pacing and screaming, on the verge of losing my mind. Various thoughts of suicide raced through my mind. The only thing that really kept me from taking out myself was the Holy

Spirit. Torment wasn't only confined to me, but it affected my wife, as well. I had to seek counseling and take anti-depressants to deal with this. None of it worked."

When he'd come home from getting high, I could see the disappointment, anger and hurt. He'd cry out loud because he did not want to be like this. So, when he went out, I would go look for him. I went into drug spots and literally pulled him out. I put myself in a lot of dangerous places and situations. I never realized how dangerous that whole environment was at the time. All I knew in my heart was that he did not want to be like that. The only way I could help him was to go and get him. This is love, right? He needed me!

The start of his fall was when he lost his first job as a carpenter's apprentice. He was devastated. He'd always prided himself on being a man who took care of his family. That was his definition of a man. His mind took him back to how he solved "being the man of the house" the last time he went to prison. Although he was saved and understood Scripture, he still had that street mentality when it came to taking care of his family. I constantly encouraged him that

God would open a door, but that it would not be in Bernard's timing.

Bernard wrote me a letter about him being in prison and how that whole dynamic breaks a person. This caused him to fight harder once he got home in order for him not to be entangled by a system that was designed to strip him of his manhood any longer. It is how they broke the slaves. That is exactly how prison was. It demeans you. Your life is totally in the hands of someone else who couldn't care less about you.

The prison system is designed to break a person down so that they have no self-esteem and no self-worth. Being a part of the Nation of Islam gave him a sense of manhood and identity. It taught the downtrodden and defenseless Black people a thorough knowledge of God and of themselves. It put them on the road to independence with a superior culture and higher civilization than they had previously experienced. These teachings, coupled with his street knowledge, were the driving force behind him taking the role of husband seriously. It was his responsibility to take care of home "by any means necessary."

What was he *fighting* for, though? His *perception* of what it meant to be a husband, or reality?

Because this kind of thinking was so engrained in him, once Bernard lost his job, he became vulnerable. He fell into that trap of wanting to have control of his life and he pushed back against everything that had been done to him. I guess this was his way of going against the system that he was now free from.

For him, losing his job and having to depend on his wife was just as demeaning as being in jail. He had to find a way to rectify that and be the man he felt the system had deprived him of becoming.

This was the way his conditioned mindset was able to get a foothold. Since we married so quickly after his release, Bernard had not dealt with the reality of being in prison versus being free. He had just spent eight and a half years in prison prior to us getting married. Before that, he had served a separate eight years.

In total, he'd served sixteen and a half years in prison since he was thirteen. In a study done by the BBC on May 1, 2018, "Longer and harsher prison sentences can mean that prisoners' personalities will be changed in ways that make their reintegration difficult."

Bernard had no option but to adapt to having no space to call his own. He also always had to be defensive, for his own safety. All this fed into the street mentality he still had. Becoming a Christian was the start of his transformation. However, he didn't give himself time to break that old way of thinking so that he could function properly once home.

When he lost his job, he went back to school for heating and cooling. The school was in the area where he used to run the streets. Of course, he started hanging around old friends. Unfortunately, they were selling weed. He started selling drugs for a moment, and that exposure eventually sucked him all the way back in.

He knew that he used drugs in the past to fill a void in his life. He couldn't understand why he would go back to it now that he was married. He had more than he ever had in his life at this point. Bernard didn't just have material things; he had finances, security and the freedom to do things without hiding.

Reading a letter that he wrote me as I was putting things together for his book helped me understand what it was that caused him to go back to it all.

"As I looked in the Word, a test would soon follow. It knocked me to the ground, which made my faith seem hollow. 'What's going on, Lord? I can't stand on my own strength.' The Lord replied, 'Now you are learning, my son. So, a gift He sent in the form of a rushing mighty wind and clothing tongues of fire that sat upon this young man took my spirit higher. This is that in which was promised in the latter days to come. You are sealed to redemption. You belong to me, my son.'"

I realized that one of the things that caused the drugs to have a stronghold on his life again was that he was standing in his own strength. He thought that, because he was saved, he could be around the same people with ran with in his past. Initially, it wasn't an issue. That was until he allowed them to convert him by selling the drugs versus him converting them to follow him in walking with the Lord.

Romans 2:3 says, *"How shall we escape if we ignore so great a salvation?"* That's when he walked away by disregarding, paying little attention to, or slighting the very thing that had brought him true freedom.

Sounds familiar!

One day when he was hanging with his friends, I happened to drive by the area, before I knew about the crack. I asked him to come home. I started telling him this was no longer who he was, and that God had a better plan for him. He got so mad at me. For the first and last time, he literally cursed me out and told me to go home. I was so hurt that I cried all the way home.

Once home, he was in tears and apologized to me. Looking back, I believe that's when it started. He had never acted that way toward me. I wasn't afraid of him, but it did break my heart. I didn't grow up around cursing, so to have someone who I thought loved me openly disrespect me felt like I'd been stabbed in the heart. All I knew was that I loved him and he loved me.

Putting my hands through open windows to open doors to drug houses, sitting outside and honking my horn until he came out, and making transactions with drug dealers to put my husband out of their spot became the norm for me.

Sometimes, he would drop me off at work and leave me to find a way home on my own. One time, he left me at a store, I believe, so he could go get high. I had to walk home. He also left me at his mom's house one time, and I had to take the bus. I was too embarrassed to ask for a ride home.

Sometimes, when he'd come home from doing drugs, I would just have to hold him because he would be shivering and crying. One thing he did ask me during one of those moments was, "Do you think any drug addict desires to be a drug addict?" Of course, I did not know the answer to that.

He said, "If you knew the pain that comes along with that, not just the physical pain with what is being done to the body, but the mental pain, the torment that comes along with it—who would really want that?"

With addicts, that first high is like the utopia of whatever you can feel. It's that desire to get that first high again that drives the addict to do it repeatedly.

The after-effects that Bernard had are hard to explain. However, having experienced it firsthand, I understand his comment that no drug addict wakes up every day wanting to be a drug addict because it is literally tormenting. Seeing the urge for drugs on his face was like watching a movie. It was as if I saw his facial features change into an image that was nothing like my husband. He would become very agitated and mean. It wasn't to the point of harming me, but he didn't want to hear what I had to say. After he got high, there was another metamorphosis. The one time he got high at home, he was smoking the pipe while he was in the bathtub, crying at the same time. It was like he wanted to stop, but he couldn't. He would sometimes hide in the closet after getting high because he became very paranoid. I assume it was due to the mental effects of the drug. There were also times when I had to hold him while he was shaking. I had to rock him like a baby for hours to calm him down.

The one thing I can say about being married to someone with an addiction is that you really are dealing with two different personalities. My husband was one person in front of others, and he was someone different when no one was looking but me. People didn't see the torment that he went through to function daily, even through the effects of the chemicals and toxins.

He would get high, rest for a day, then get high again the next day. It was literally back to back to back. Yet, he continued to work and live in such a way that the addiction could not be detected if he didn't tell you about it. He was a functional addict!

Bernard would go from taking my car to get high, and leaving me to find a way home, to handing me his check to keep him from spending it on drugs. He did not want to have money on him even though, when the desire to get drugs hit him, he would sell anything in his possession. But in his heart, he really wanted to do right. He really wanted to be a man I could honor and respect. What he could do, or tried to do, or was doing, he did in his own strength. The spiritual struggle with him was letting go of the fight and allowing the Holy Spirit to do a work in him.

By Any Means Necessary

So far, you have seen glimpses of a pattern in my life that brought me to this point—*my own addiction.*

The question really is whose and what was the addiction in the marriage? Was it the drugs, or was it me having my dreams fulfilled at any cost? In the actual drug addiction, you can see the physical effects of what happened to Bernard. But the effects of my addiction were much more subtle. I didn't even realize I had one until it was almost too late.

Everything I did was under the disguise of "love." To love someone is a good thing, right? If so, something good should come out of it, right? Not necessarily, especially when the motive behind what you are doing comes from a place of selfishness.

What's the motivation behind your choices? That is your why. Why do you do the things you do? Is it to help others or to help yourself?

One thing Bernard constantly told me was to never allow his actions to change the person God had created me to be and the woman he married.

"Don't change who you are, what you believe, what you're doing or not doing, for me. Even though I fuss, even though I get upset, keep doing what you are doing. That is God using you to help me get through this."

He knew our marriage served a greater purpose than anything we could have ever imagined. God knew where he was going to be in his life. Had anyone else been in his life, they would have turned on him. They would have let him go to the streets and let the streets deal with him, as many told me I should had done.

As true as that may have been, I don't believe it should have been at the expense of him losing his life. I don't believe it should have been at the expense of me losing my mind. To have the life we both always dreamed of, it was a price we both were willing to pay. At some point, we both stopped fighting for the marriage. Instead, we fought for the image of what we thought a marriage should be. Like the first high Bernard chased after time and time again, we were committed to the marriage by any means necessary! We had an unspoken allegiance to make the naysayers out to be liars.

One Friday night, Bernard didn't come home. He called me for help. To make a point of what this was doing to me, I went to the drug dealer Saturday morning and pawned my wedding ring. I thought giving up the symbol of our love would make him see how much this was hurting me. It didn't work. I did go back after a few days to get the ring without him knowing.

Oftentimes, I drove around all night, trying to find his car. I knew his spots. The drug dealers knew me. Some would let me in, while others would simply send him out. In addition to not getting any sleep, I also started overeating. I gained almost fifty pounds. I am so thankful that God gave me a boss who I was able to talk to about it. So, if I needed to sleep in a bit, take a day off or leave early to find him, she understood. She was sympathetic for me because I still did my job faithfully.

When he was high, I could sometimes get him to come home. But once he saw that I would come looking for him, the manipulation began. A few times, he called me, saying that he needed money for the dealers to release him. In the middle of the night, I would get hundreds of dollars from the bank to bring to him.

After giving him money for the drugs one night, he went into the drug house to pay his debt, or so I thought. Once I realized he wasn't coming back to the car, I went to the door of the house and asked for my husband. I asked why they would give an addict credit for drugs. The drug dealer then schooled me on the game Bernard had run on me. Bernard would run out of money and have me bring more so he could continue to get high.

I was so mad that, once I found him a block away, I drove my car on the curb where he was walking, jumped out and used curse words I never knew I could say. I also think I bumped him with the car when I jumped the curb. That was the last time he asked me to bring him money. Once home, he realized how angry I was, and he begged me not to come looking for him anymore, under any circumstances.

I used to have a glass of wine, socially. At job-related functions, a glass of wine is not a big deal. But I found myself drinking to go to sleep so I wouldn't go look for Bernard. Otherwise, I would be up all night, worrying about him and wondering what was going on. I would literally drink a whole bottle of wine. I was trying to escape the reality of my choices. I did not have a drug addiction, but did I not also have an addiction? Who *really* had the addiction?

As much as I wanted Bernard to stop, I soon understood the compulsive nature that drives an addiction.

Even though Bernard didn't steal anything physically from our home, he sold every personal possession. He pawned his original wedding ring and sold every cell phone he had. I kept insurance on his cell phones. But after several claims within a short period of time, the cell phone company wouldn't allow the coverage for any phones under my name. He also pawned gym shoes, coats and other jewelry.

But to keep up with the image of marriage, I kept buying everything he ended up selling. Everyone knows I love to dress and look like a lady. There was no way my man *wasn't* going to compliment me when we were together. I may have never verbalized this, but my actions were done all under the camouflage of love, even though I was enabling him to continue in his enslavement.

I opened joint credit cards accounts with Mickey Shorr and Home Depot, which he used to purchase things only to sell them. The first time, I didn't know what he was doing—until, one day, he came home with his truck stripped of its sound equipment from Mickey Shorr. I should have known better.

The period of him not working caused a lot of stress on me. I had to carry the bills at home, along with additional expenses.

But I had to keep up the image and the lifestyle I was accustomed to, which kept us in debt. I could not, and would not, let my credit score go below 750. I had never lived a life of lack. I wouldn't let anyone know how hard this time really was for us. I always had to look the part. To put it another way, I had to fake it until I made it!

Looking back on it now, he did steal the funds that could have been used for our home.

Not only did I have to care for my husband, but my nephew Chris was also living with us at the start of our marriage. I don't remember anything about me being a "mother" to him during this period, until he and Bernard began to butt heads. Once Bernard got his heating and cooling certification, he got a job as a maintenance tech at an apartment complex, which allowed us to live on the property for free. As the head of the household, Bernard set rules for Chris that Chris didn't like. Chris knew about his uncle's addiction, and he saw how it affected me.

There were many arguments, but one escalated into a physical altercation. Bernard wouldn't have hit Chris, but I had to step in to keep Chris from stabbing him. Chris had to go! I understood Bernard's stance, but I also saw how the effects of the addiction, and my choices, had built up resentment in Chris' heart for both me and Bernard. I was conflicted on whether to stand with my husband or Chris.

I was up many nights and I cried constantly at having my heart torn between the two. The first few days, I got a hotel room for Chris and I to stay at until I figured out my plan. I also had Chris stay with one of his classmates for a few weeks. Having to ask a stranger for help, and explain the reason, was one of the most hurtful, humiliating things I've ever done. Not only was I failing God, but I was failing my nephew.

Finally, my mom chose to move closer to me so that Chris could live with her. That way, his schooling wouldn't be interrupted. Was I right to have put my marriage first? Should I have walked away and taken care of my nephew instead? What exactly was I fighting for?

Now that it was just Bernard and me in the house, things got worse. Bernard had been more conscious of his behavior while Chris lived with us. However, once Chris was gone, Bernard didn't care how he behaved. He was the man of the house and, whatever his behavior, I now depended on him for the roof over our heads.

At this point, the addiction went from a few days out of the week to every day! He made sure the bills were paid, but whatever extra money he had went to drugs. You may wonder how he was able to keep his job after all-night binges. There were days when he couldn't work. So, he would go to the ER for detox and get a letter from the ER to take to work. He made sure to get a doctor's note that he was seen in the ER, but the note never stated the cause of treatment. Also, whenever his employer conducted a random drug test, he would take niacin to keep the drugs from being detected in his urine. He had it all planned, and he almost got away with it.

One evening while on a call, he was out getting high. A pipe broke in one of the apartments on the property and he didn't respond. His supervisor called me several times, looking for him. I covered for him, which had become my normal response. I told the supervisor that I didn't know where he was, so I didn't lie altogether.

Once I did get in contact with him, I found that he had gone to the ER to detox and get a doctor's note. He was so good with this that he thought he was covered. But, this time, he gave his job the wrong information from the ER, which showed that the ER visit was for detox. They quickly ordered a drug test, which he failed.

Forced to move out of the apartment complex, we had to move into his mother's basement. Since moving out of my parents' house in 1998, I never had to stay with anyone. This was hard for me. Now, in addition to having to deal with the addiction, I had to follow the rules his mother set for her household. The once loving relationship she and I had was now full of tension. I no longer saw her as my best friend or godmother, but as Bernard's mother. Wanting to love and respect my husband was hard when he was constantly reminded by his family at this point of their displeasure with what he was doing.

I could no longer hide the reality of how bad the addiction had become.

I became very angry with his family. As much as they would speak about what he was doing, and my part in enabling him, they would often use him to do handyman work for basically pennies. Then, they would act almost surprised or ignore the fact that he took the money to get high. They saw what he was doing and what I was doing since I chose to stay. But they didn't see the part they played. This made me mad as hell at them all! Even though my choice to stay was selfish, their misuse of him was, as well. We all had a part to play, not just me!

After a few months, I knew we had to get out of there for our sanity's sake! Thankfully, we were able to move back into the apartment I had before we got married. He was able to find another job as a maintenance tech, overseeing purchases for the property with a Home Depot credit card account.

Being the good wife that I was, I tried to get him to let me keep the card. I would go with him when he needed items, or I would get them for him. I was willing to jeopardize my job by leaving work to shop just to keep him out of trouble. This shows just how lost I was by the illusion I created in my mind.

Time proved, again, that I can't make choices for someone else and expect them to comply.

After a few months on the job, he saw how he could use the card to purchase items to sell for drugs, which he did twice. The second time, we didn't have the money to cover what he'd spent. Bernard was afraid he would go to jail, so I met with his supervisor. I explained his addiction, and he was fired. His employer kept his last paycheck to pay off the credit card account. No criminal charges were filed.

You would think I would draw the line in what I would do "in the name of love" seeing that I wasn't getting back the same degree of love in return. If he loved me, why wouldn't he stop?

Love is an action word, but those acts must come from an open heart, not self-centeredness.

My obsession continued with me sitting in the car for hours while he did odd jobs to make sure he wouldn't use the money for drugs. Those claims on his truck caught up with him, and I was almost charged with insurance fraud because the policy was in my name. Then, there was the time we stole back his truck from a dealer after Bernard had sold it to him for drugs! It was like a scene out of a movie.

Bernard and I drove around looking for the truck one night. When we saw it, we sat on the corner to see if anyone would come out of the house it was parked in front of before we made our move. After a few minutes, I slowly drove up to the truck, and Bernard jumped out with the extra key we had. He started the truck, and we both sped off before the dealer knew the truck was gone.

I am thankful to God that I did not get sucked into the drugs because I felt compelled to go after him. I had to look for him. I had to save him. I know now that it was a mixture of loving him, and an inward thing pulling me. This was fueled by the seeds of my childhood and the incremental choices I made over my life. I was addicted to trying to keep everything together. I was addicted to looking after him, to the point that I lost who I was in the process.

Unfair Advantage

Because I knew his heart was to be delivered and set free to do the things God had called him to do, God showed me how to separate my husband from the addiction. God showed me how to love my husband yet hate the addiction. I knew his heart. This wasn't the time for me to leave. My position was to constantly remind him of who God had called him to be. I was there to remind him that he was not defined by what he did, but by what God had called him to be. He needed to walk it out. His identity was not defined by the addiction.

After a year of living with the addiction, I learned how to recognize when the drugs were calling him. Beer was his trigger. After I stopped looking for him, I would try to distract him from going out. In the beginning, to my shame, I used sex to entice him to stay home. It worked for a moment, until I realized that I had to look out for myself. I didn't know what he was into while getting high. He could have been with other women or sharing crack pipes with total strangers. I started hiding the car keys, until he reminded me that his past life included stealing cars.

One of the most painful parts about this season was that every insecurity I had from my childhood manifested and became a stronghold, which took me years after his death to get free from.

"Why don't you love me enough to stop?" was my heart's cry.

I never asked him this out loud because I knew it wasn't a fair request to make of him. His desire to be free had to go beyond me. He had to do it for himself.

I questioned everything about myself and magnified every bad thought about my identity. I made excuses as to why he didn't love me enough to stop. I always rationalized that I'd rather he'd cheat with a woman. At least that way, I could see my competition. I could be better, look better and treat him better than the woman who drew him away from me. But the hard reality kept hitting me. How could I compete with an addiction? It satisfied him in a way I never could, but he kept telling me that he loved me. This wasn't love. If he loved me, he would put the drugs down! In my mind, what I was doing for *him* was love!

Like I said earlier, I was dealing with two different personalities. God showed me how to love my husband, yet, hate the addiction. Bernard, the man I married, had a big heart. He did anything he could to help others. The addiction side of him was horrible though! When he was high, I didn't know him. He lied, manipulated me, used me and made me feel insecure in the one relationship I had built so much hope on—only to be disappointed time and time again.

Before Bernard passed, friends and family called me dumb and stupid. "Why are you staying with this man?" they asked me. "You're enabling him!" they told me. "You crazy!" some of my friends said. "You need to let the world deal with him!" so many people told me. But, that's not Scripture. In Scripture, it talks about what happens when you turn somebody over to the world. What hope do they have? This point may be debatable, but my position was to allow him to deal with the consequences of his choices. I didn't want to enable him, but to love him through it, regardless of the views and comments of others. I was supposed to be able to minister to my husband.

Marriage is ministry. It's not just for me to be satisfied or for him to be satisfied. Marriage isn't just to live together and have fun. When I said, "for better or for worse," which is subjective to individual interpretation or circumstances, it encompassed everything—except for sacrificing Marietta to save Bernard. My "worse" could look totally different in someone else's eyes. I had to come to the realization that I didn't have the ability to save him. I didn't have to give up who God created me to be in the process of Bernard's journey. Ministry builds. The only thing ministry may tear down or dismantle is our selfish desires and will. We need the help of God in every area of our lives. "I do" should complement you, not change you.

It's not like I was innocent from bad behavior during this period. There were times when Bernard was shivering in the bed, asking me just to hold him. I would say, "No, I don't want to hold you." I would curse at him, hoping that my acting out of character would wake him up to how he was breaking my heart. Even when he wasn't high, I allowed my mind to go back to the times when he was. I wouldn't, I couldn't, get past that. At that point, he really needed me to minister to him. But I couldn't because he no longer looked like the man of my dreams!

God protected me from a lot of things. I was ignorant. Bernard's addiction was killing him mentally, physically and spiritually. My addiction of trying to keep everything together, and trying to present this idea of a marriage, of a relationship, of a home, was just as detrimental to me mentally, physically and spiritually.

'Til Death Do Us Part

You would think that after Bernard passed, the torment of his drug addiction and its effects on my life ended. But I went through another phase of torment after his passing. It was the torment of depression, anxiety, sleepless nights, thoughts of suicide and guilt that I didn't do enough to stop his drug use. I understood that Bernard had made his choices. I could not understand why toward the last six to nine months of his life, I simply had peace. No one could have told me how our story would have ended. The peace I had was solid. I no longer feared the addiction and what it may do to Bernard. I trusted God for his life. This is where the torment came from. I trusted God that Bernard was going to be alright, but he died! What in the hell happened? I felt like my hopes were built up only to have the foundation of my faith crumble around me. I could not understand why God would allow me to invest in something that would be taken away from me. The agony of not only his and my choices haunted me, but now the feeling of being forsaken by God haunted me! If He let me down, who or what did I have left?

I started writing this book during this addiction, thinking it was going to be a journal of what I went through. I thought it would be a journal of what we went through together and, at the end this glorious triumphant ending, he was going to make it through. God blessed him and he was going to be on fire for the Lord.

Many times, in the desire to get married, we neglect to take a realistic view of the life following, "I do." As I look back, I never focused on us living happily ever after with kids and a dog. All I envisioned was us doing ministry together. Again, I was using a "good thing" to justify the choices I had made earlier in my life. From getting married too soon, to not allowing Bernard to acclimate himself to life outside the prison system, my decisions yielded an unexpected outcome. Coupled with insecurities from my childhood, my desire to please everyone played a part in how I thought marriage was supposed to be. It's like looking at life through broken eyeglasses. Everything you view from this position is distorted and fractured, even if there is some reality behind it.

I guess I had peace that everything was okay because it was, though not the way I wanted it to be.

Had we gotten married too soon? Had I opened the door to his drug addiction by drinking champagne on our wedding night? Should we have moved from Detroit as he requested, which I'd talked him out of? Why hadn't I heard him leave that last night? Was his last altercation with the dealer regarding our car my fault, in that he knew I would be mad if he didn't come back with the car? Had I created an environment that aided in his continued use?

These thoughts plagued me daily! The whys of what I did and what I did not do tormented me. I asked, "God, what's up? What happened?" I began to lose hope.

I did not want counsel or prayer from anyone. As much as I knew the Word of God, I was convinced that I messed up so badly that God no longer heard my prayers. I'd prayed for my husband and he still died. John 5:16 says, "The effectual fervent prayer of a righteous man availeth much." I felt as if I was no longer righteous or in right standing with God.

One of Bernard's favorite stories was about Abraham, how he hoped against hope. It was almost like I did not have hope anymore. I know I prayed for Bernard, believed God and had a peace about it. Yet, he ended up dead! How could this be? I could not understand.

To add to this, I battled with thoughts of losing every man I had truly loved: my dad, Renard, and now, Bernard. I labeled myself "The Black Widow," which created a whole new dysfunctional thought pattern. Who would love me, knowing my past?

Everything about me no longer existed. The confident, bold, passionate woman of God no longer existed. I had given so much to keeping up the image of the marriage, I was lost. I literally died. After his death, it was hard to live outside of the identity I created as the wife, the protector, the one who kept everything together. I was so good at it that my own mother didn't even know about the addiction until the day of his death.

Now that I was left to face the reality of my choices, I did the very thing I'd tried to keep Bernard from doing. I became even more angry and bitter at family, friends and the Church. This was a defense mechanism I unknowingly used to keep from looking at my responsibility for why I was where I was at this point in my life.

Having to make some sense of all this, I created and published some of his writings and created a non-profit foundation in his name, The WBJ Foundation. We did one fundraiser, but most of the money came from his insurance policy, which I freely squandered. I didn't feel right profiting or living good off his death. I did give one scholarship, but I couldn't keep the foundation together alone. I tried for years, until I realized this was something *I did* rather than seeking God for direction.

A good thing isn't always a God thing!

I would be at church, silently screaming in my heart. No one sensed the pain and torment I was experiencing. Some days, I felt that if I had a gun in my hand, I would just blow my head off. It seemed like everyone else around me received prayer but me. I felt like no one gave a damn if I kept serving Sunday after Sunday.

Even when I tried to date, I kept looking for men to rescue me. I came to that realization when the insecurities from my marriage presented themselves, such as abandonment in the form of not keeping your word. I would explain my issues to them and ask them to walk with me as I tried to heal. This was an unfair request to ask someone who was just getting to know me. It was unfair to ask those men to carry my baggage. They also had to watch me go from one extreme to another when something they did brought feelings up from my hurt past. Bernard was dead, so I couldn't express the pain of what he put me through to him. I ended up making the men I dated pay for something they had nothing to do with.

I found myself in the same situation as my marriage. I tried to do things to show that I was worthy of their love. "I'm a good cook. I keep a clean house. I'll help you with your business." None of the three relationships I tried lasted. I think the term for it is they "ghosted" me. I don't blame them because I was asking them to do something only God could do. I was also asking them to love me, when I no longer knew what love looked like because I no longer loved myself. You can't ask someone else to love you when you don't love yourself. You will always see the love given to you from a distorted view. It will be ever changing and not stable.

This was never the person I was prior to getting married, but God wanted to heal the remnants of the broken Marietta, which I had given away.

As hard as this felt at the time, this was the start of my healing.

Life After Death

Why should anyone pity me? Were they responsible for what happened to me? Did they have anything to do with the choices I had made? Why should I look for people to do for me what only God could do, which was to forgive me and heal my broken heart? I was blaming others for something they had no clue they did. They had nothing to do with my plight. I created many false illusions in my mind to keep me from looking at myself. I was unknowingly trying to make others my savior—the ones responsible for helping me out of my mess—as I was trying to be for Bernard.

I had to take the hard journey out of playing the victim. Even while Bernard was alive, I played it like a fiddle. "Why don't you love me?" played constantly in my heart, without me realizing that it wasn't his or anyone else's responsibility to love me. I now had to learn to do one of the hardest things I'd ever had to do: learn to love myself. One would think that this shouldn't be a hard thing to do. But keep in mind, I was a people pleaser from childhood. Putting others before me was the norm. I took pride in being an administrator. I felt it was my calling to make others look good, but I did it at my own expense and detriment.

On this journey of self-love, I had to go to important people in my life and ask them to forgive me. I had to tell others what they'd done to hurt me. This was an important process because it showed me that my perspective of those relationships was all wrong. It wasn't reality. I stayed in a victim mentality for so long because of what I felt my husband, and those who knew about his addiction, did to me or didn't do for me. This mentality wouldn't allow me to see what I had done to others. It also gave them a pass to hurt me. God showed me through this exercise that I was used to not confronting my choices as a defense mechanism. If I could put my hurt from not being able to help Bernard, and disappointments of me not getting the marriage I'd dreamed of on them, then I wouldn't feel them. My mindset was that those I confronted were just as much enablers as I was. They owed me an apology for walking away from us. It was everyone else's burden to bear with me.

I had to ask God to forgive me for my actions in my marriage. God often used Bernard to encourage me not to allow his actions to change who I was. I chose to do what I did, and it wasn't even Bernard's fault. I also had to ask God to forgive me for allowing anger to distort how I felt about different people who were once dear to me. I realized that I was holding people hostage in my heart over something they had no clue about, which was taking up space in my heart. I couldn't love anyone, not even myself.

In doing this, I realized that I was looking for others to satisfy the emptiness in my heart and soul in ways that only God could. I had to return to my first love and cast my cares, disappointments, anxieties, hurts and loneliness on God.

This also helped me to truly recognize God's love. Most of my life, prior to getting married, was good. I never lacked and things came easy for me. Whatever I put my hands to prospered. I never had to struggle in any area. So, knowing all I had done in the name of love, to have God's love with open arms, is beyond humbling. Once I began to see all I had done, and how it was my fault, God could have left me to wallow in the mess I created. But He loved me through it. The revelation of each area uncovered where I was at fault and was accompanied with love and a peace that I can't put into words.

At times, I wanted to end my life and give up. But God wouldn't allow it. He always sent simple reminders in a song, or time for me to look at creation and its beauty, about just how much He loves me. Even in those times when I was mad at Him for my choices, He was always in pursuit of me. There was so much more He had for me to do. I had allowed my voice to be silenced from sharing with others. But my prayer eventually became, *"And for me, that utterance may be given unto me, that I may open my mouth boldly, to make known the mystery of the gospel"* (Ephesians 6:19).

Embracing God's love for me allowed me to forgive and love myself again. I no longer lived from a victim mentality. I've moved forward.

Nothing I went through speaks of my strength as a woman of God, daughter, friend, sister or wife. There were so many flaws to who I was during my marriage that none of those titles identified what I had become.

I am a woman of God who loves God with all her heart, yet I went against His instructions at times. And He loved me through it.

I am a daughter, who selflessly cares for my parent. But sometimes, I run on empty with little to nothing to give. But God gives strength in these times of weakness.

I am a friend and sister you can call at any time, day or night. I'm there, but I sometimes overextend myself, wanting to please everyone, to the point of resenting the very ones I put myself out for.

I was a wife who gave my all, to the point of losing who I was in the process. But God restored everything I lost, mentally, physically and spiritually. As a matter of fact, those identity markers are just titles to express the hand of God in each area of the gardens in my life God has planted me in to tend, cultivate and nurture for His glory!

About the Author

Marietta Mills Jones is a beacon of inspiration, an advocate for personal growth, and a testament to overcoming adversity. As a licensed minister and ordained elder, Marietta's holistic approach to personal transformation addresses spiritual, emotional, and practical challenges. She openly shares her vulnerabilities, setting a powerful example for others on a similar growth journey.

Marietta's impact extends beyond her spiritual role to include authorship, motivational speaking, and philanthropy. Her collaboration on the book "In My Own Words" and the award-winning "Married to an Addiction" reflect her commitment to sharing life wisdom. Marietta's extensive portfolio demonstrates her dedication to empowering a broader audience.

Recognized on various media platforms, Marietta's presence includes appearances on "Good News with Greg Davis" and features in esteemed publications in and outside the United States. At the heart of Marietta's journey lies the reminder that authenticity, resilience, and story-sharing lead to true purpose. Online fundraisers through 4Ever Thankful, LLC, have raised thousands of dollars for non-profits.

Marietta's online presence, inspirational blog, and social media engagement amplifies her message of empowerment and faith. Available for speaking engagements, she showcases her commitment to creating positive ripples in lives.

As CEO of 4Ever Thankful, LLC, Marietta provides inspirational content fostering gratitude and empowerment. Her life story is a testament to resilience, growth, and the transformative power of personal experiences, making her a role model dedicated to uplifting and inspiring others.

Scan the QR code below to access the video series that inspired *Married 2 an Addiction*—a deeper look into faith, healing, and hope beyond addiction.

For speaking engagements or interviews, visit www.4everthankful.com or email mariettamillsjones@4everthankful.com. You can also connect with Marietta Mills Jones on Facebook, Instagram, YouTube and LinkedIn.

4EVER *Thankful* LLC

www.4EverThankful.com

www.ingramcontent.com/pod-product-compliance
Lightning Source LLC
Chambersburg PA
CBHW071231290326
41931CB00037B/2677